NATIONAL GEOGRAPHIC

LIFE SCIENCE

Plant Power

KATE BOEHM NYQUIST

PICTURE CREDITS:
Cover: ©Clifton Carr/Minden Pictures. Pages 1, 19 (low) © Clifton Carr/Minden Pictures; pages 2–3 © Jane Grushow/Grant Heilman Photography, Inc.; page 4 © Robert P. Falls; page 5 (top), page 11 (top) PhotoDisc®; page 5 (low) © Bill Beatty; page 6 © Bob and Clara Calhoun/Bruce Coleman, Inc./Picture Quest; page 7 (background) © Dorling Kindersley; page 7 © Winterthur Museum; page 8 (left) © Barry Runk/Grant Heilman Photography, Inc.; pages 8 (right), 9 (top) © Runk/Schoenberger/Grant Heilman Photography, Inc.; page 9 (low) © Len Rue, Jr.; page 10 © Hans Reinhard/OKAPIA/Photo Researchers, Inc.; page 11 (mid.) © Jung Aribert/Earth Scenes, © Gerald L. Moore; page 12 © Galen Rowell/CORBIS; page 13 (top right, low background) Comstock; page 13 (top right) U.S. Government/Library of Congress; page 13 (low right) © Robert Pickett/CORBIS; pages 14, 16 Precision Graphics; page 15 Stephen Dalton/Animals Animals; page 17 (top left) © Visuals Unlimited; page 17 (top right) Patti Murray/Animals Animals; page 17 (low) © Andrew McRobb/Dorling Kindersley; page 18 © Michael P. Gadomski/Photo Researchers, Inc.; page 19 (top left) © John Kaprielian/Photo Researchers, Inc.; page 19 (top right) © Stephen P. Parker/Photo Researchers, Inc.; pages 20–21 © Mark Moffett/Minden Pictures; page 22 (left) © E. R. Degginger/Bruce Coleman, Inc.; page 22 (right) © Diana Z. Leskovac; page 23 NASA; pages 24 (top and mid.), 25 (top right, mid-right, low left) Wildlife Art, Ltd.; page 24 (low) Lynn Johnson; page 25 (top left) The Picture Cube; page 25 (low mid.) Mary E. Eaton; page 26 New York Botanical Garden; page 27 © Mark O. Theissen/NGS; page 29 © Lloyd Wolf/NGS; page 30 © Frans Lanting/Minden Pictures.

Back cover: (top to bottom) Digital Stock, Chris Johns/NGS Image Collection, Digital Stock, PhotoDisc®; National Cancer Institute/SPL/Photo Researchers, Inc.

Cover photo: Agave plant

Produced through the worldwide resources of the National Geographic Society, John M. Fahey, Jr., President and Chief Executive Officer; Gilbert M. Grosvenor, Chairman of the Board; Nina D. Hoffman, Executive Vice President and President, Books and School Publishing.

PREPARED BY NATIONAL GEOGRAPHIC SCHOOL PUBLISHING
Ericka Markman, Senior Vice President; Steve Mico, Editorial Director; Barbara Seeber, Editorial Manager; Lynda McMurray, Amy Sarver, Project Editors; Jim Hiscott, Design Manager; Karen Thompson, Art Director; Kristin Hanneman, Illustrations Manager; Diana Bourdrez, Tom DiGiovanni, Ruth Goldberg, Diana Z. Leskovac, Anne Whittle, Photo Editors; Christine Higgins, Photo Coordinator; Matt Wascavage, Manager of Publishing Services; Sean Philpotts, Production Coordinator.

Production: Clifton M. Brown III, Manufacturing and Quality Control.

CONSULTANT/REVIEWER
Rebecca L. Johnson, Biologist/Science writer, Sioux Falls, South Dakota

PROGRAM DEVELOPMENT
Kate Boehm Nyquist

BOOK DESIGN
3r1 Group

Published by the National Geographic Society
1145 17th Street, N.W.
Washington, D.C. 20036-4688

ISBN: 0-7922-8860-2

Printed in Canada.

Garden sculpture, Cornwall, England

Contents

Plants to the Rescue

Appalachian Mountains, North Carolina

It was spring 1810, deep in the southern Appalachians. A Cherokee girl held her aching stomach and cried in pain. What could she do?

Cherokee tradition provided the answer. Native Americans knew how to use the forest as their pharmacy. The knowledge of how to use plants to cure illness was passed down from generation to generation. For stomachaches, the Cherokee made a medicine from the roots of the goldenseal plant. The girl took her medicine and began to feel better.

Without plants, humans would not survive. We depend on plants for food, medicine, clothing, and even the oxygen we breathe. Think of the plants all around you. Tree limbs sway in the breeze. Colorful flowers line paths in the park. Weeds sprout up in empty lots. Plants are everywhere.

This is a book about the green world that grows silently around us. We have learned how to use plants in many ways. We are beginning to understand that there are many more possibilities. So dig into the world of plants, where dirt is good and green is golden.

Goldenseal plant

Chapter 1

Function and Form

Green Machines

Horsetail plants

In the foothills of the Appalachians, a settler's family enjoyed a hearty meal. Soon the children headed down to a nearby stream. But they weren't going for a swim.

They were on their way to pick horsetail plants. Their mother needed tough scrubbing brushes to clean the cooking pot, and there was a good supply at the edge of the stream. Horsetails, which are among the most ancient plants, probably were used as cleaning brushes by many people. These plants have been around for millions of years. Giant horsetails once stood in vast forests that covered much of Earth's land surface.

From the tough brush of a horsetail to the soft petals of a rose, plants come in many different shapes and sizes. Plants grow almost everywhere—from low country rivers to high mountain slopes. Even though they can be very different, plants all require light, water, nutrients, and carbon dioxide. They share many of the same parts that help them meet these needs.

Antique iron pot

The orange part of a carrot is a taproot.

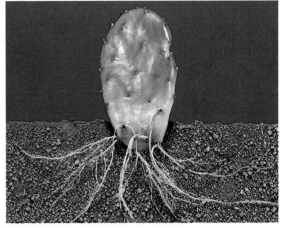
A prickly pear cactus has a fibrous root system.

Roots Anchor and Absorb

What parts of a plant do you like to eat? If you like to chomp on a carrot or gobble down forkfuls of sweet potatoes, then you're a root-eating kid. Roots are important structures that do many things for a plant.

There are two main types of root systems. A **taproot** system has one main root that is thicker than the others. This taproot grows straight down into the soil. A carrot is a good example of a plant that has a taproot. The other type of system is a **fibrous root system**. Plants with this kind of root system, such as grasses, have several roots of about the same size. These roots spread out in many directions.

No matter what kind of roots a plant has, every root does certain things. Roots anchor a plant in place. When the wind blows hard and a plant bends and sways, but doesn't fall over, you know the roots are doing their job. Roots also can store food for a plant. When you eat a carrot, you are eating the plant's stored food.

Another important job of roots is to absorb, or take in, water and minerals from the soil. Look at the seedling pictured on the next page. The threadlike hairs coming off the main root are called root hairs. These hairy extensions increase the surface area of the root. This allows it to take in more water and minerals.

Root hairs sprout from a radish seedling.

Stems Support and Carry

A beaver bites and pulls and tears out pieces of wood. Finally, the tree begins to lean. Timber! After years of growing straight into the air, the tree slowly tips and falls to the ground. The beaver digs into the tasty bark. This huge stem makes great meals for many days.

Trees and shrubs have **woody stems**. These stems grow strong and thick over many years in order to support big plants. Smaller plants have softer, more flexible stems.

Stems provide support to plants. In most plants, this means the stem holds the leaves up so they can get enough sunlight. The other important function of stems is to transport water and minerals from the roots to the leaves and to transport food from the leaves to other parts of the plant. Tubelike structures inside the stems carry these necessities.

A beaver gnaws on a tree trunk.

Leaves Produce Food

You may already know that almost all plants make their own food. Some plants, like the cactus, can make food in their stems. But most plants use their leaves to do this job. The substance in leaves that gives them their green color is called **chlorophyll**. Chlorophyll traps energy from sunlight. Then the important food-making process of **photosynthesis** can begin.

What's so important about photosynthesis? It not only provides plants with food but also provides us with oxygen. There are two main steps in photosynthesis. In the first step, chlorophyll traps light energy from the sun. The light energy is used to split water into oxygen and hydrogen. The oxygen goes into the air.

In the second step of photosynthesis, the hydrogen is combined with carbon dioxide to make sugar. The sugar is stored as food for the plant.

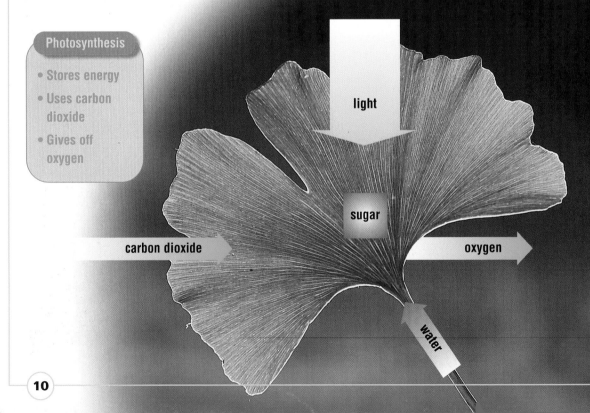

What Is Photosynthesis?

Photosynthesis

- Stores energy
- Uses carbon dioxide
- Gives off oxygen

light

sugar

carbon dioxide

oxygen

water

Remember, plant cells are alive. So, just like animals, plants need food for energy. When a plant needs its stored food, its cells may use oxygen to break apart the sugars. This gives off energy in a process called **respiration**. This energy-releasing process can happen day or night.

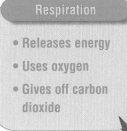

Respiration

- Releases energy
- Uses oxygen
- Gives off carbon dioxide

Thinking Like a Scientist: Observing

Some of the most important breakthroughs in science are made because of careful observations. To find out about an object, or **observe** it, you can touch it, smell it, look at it, and even listen to it.

Look at the leaves pictured on this page. Although you can't really touch them, you can learn a lot by observing them closely. Try to match the description with the picture.

Types of Leaves

Leaf	Description
Ash	a compound leaf with many small leaflets
Maple	a simple leaf with only one flat blade
Douglas fir	many needlelike leaves

How are these types of leaves alike? How are they different?

Chapter 2

Growth and Survival
Ready, Set, Grow

Giant sequoia

How "giant" is a giant sequoia? It could shade a jumbo jet. It would take a classroom of kids holding hands to encircle its trunk. It can grow taller than the Statue of Liberty.

The sequoia tree was named for a Cherokee Native American leader called Sequoyah, who created symbols to represent the Cherokee language.

Giant sequoias are among the largest and oldest living things on Earth. The trunks of these amazing trees can grow to be more than 9 meters (30 feet) across. Because of its enormous size, the giant sequoia is also known as the mammoth tree. Giant sequoias are found only in California, and most are protected in national parks. The trees can live for more than 3,000 years.

It's hard to believe that a tree as large as a sequoia can grow from a tiny seed, but that's exactly what happens. However, not all plants make seeds. For example, ferns and mosses grow from tiny structures called **spores**. But most plants are seed plants. So how do seed plants grow? How do they make seeds to form new plants?

Clusters of red spores on a fern leaf

Going to Seed

Have you ever picked up a pinecone? Such cones contain seeds for one group of seed plants, called **conifers**. The giant sequoias are conifers. Most conifers, such as pines, firs, and spruces, are also called **evergreens**. These trees don't lose their leaves in the winter. They stay green year-round. That's why we call them evergreens.

Another big group of seed plants is **flowering plants**. Flowering plants need flowers to make seeds.

Most flowers have four main parts. Let's start by thinking about a flower bud. The bud is covered with green, leaflike parts. These are called **sepals**, and they protect the bud. As the bud grows, the sepals are forced apart.

The most obvious part of a flower is usually its **petals**. The petals have scents, colors, and shapes that attract birds, bees, butterflies, and other animals to the flower. These creatures help in the seed-making process.

If you look in the center of the ring of petals, you'll usually see a **pistil**. This part of the flower produces eggs, which will be needed to make seeds.

Before seeds can be made, the eggs must combine with sperm, which is produced by **pollen**. The part of the plant that makes the pollen is called the **stamen**.

Parts of a Flower

1. Petal
2. Pistil
3. Stamen
4. Sepal

Pollen Pickup

Before a seed can form, pollen needs to be moved from a flower's stamen to a pistil in a process called **pollination**. Sometimes plants pollinate themselves, but more often pollen comes from another plant. However, most plants are rooted to one spot. How does pollen get from one plant to another?

In lots of ways! Remember that the petals of flowers are made to attract other organisms. Petals come in bright colors, and some petals even have runway-like patterns that show an insect a good place to land. When a bee lands in the middle of a flower to feed on **nectar**, pollen collects on its legs or back. The pollen may rub off onto the stamen of the next flower the bee visits.

Wind also can carry pollen from one plant to another. You may already know this if you are allergic to pollen. You can be miserable with sneezing and watery eyes when there is a lot of it in the air.

Why do you think some plants have to release large amounts of pollen?

What if...?

Bees pollinate several different types of crops in the United States. What do you think would happen if pesticides killed many of these bees?

Flower to Fruit

Once a plant gets pollen in the right place, a process called **fertilization** occurs. After landing on a pistil, pollen starts to grow a long thin tube called a pollen tube. The pollen tube grows down into the part of the pistil that has the egg cells. When sperm from the pollen travel down the tube and meet an egg, the egg is fertilized. A seed can now develop from the fertilized egg cell.

After fertilization, most parts of a flower die and fall away. The part that contained the egg cells slowly changes into a new part. This part is the **fruit**. The fruit protects the seed or seeds while they grow. Ripe fruits have seeds that can grow into new plants.

Getting Around

A fruit enjoyed by the Cherokee tribe was the persimmon. As many Cherokee children learned, this fruit tastes terrible before it is completely ripe. After ripening, persimmons taste sweet and delicious.

In late fall persimmons soften and drop to the ground. When a ripe fruit falls and starts to rot, it's performing an important job. It's helping to spread the seeds, so they can start to grow new plants.

Fertilization

1 Pollen lands on pistil

2 Pollen tube grows

3 Sperm meets egg cell to form seed

Each pair of seeds of the Norway maple has wings that act like helicopter rotors when blown off the tree.

Persimmon fruit

Seeds are spread in many ways. Some are blown about by the wind. Others are carried away. When an animal eats fruit, it may not be able to digest the seeds. What does this mean? You guessed it. The seeds get deposited in the animal's droppings.

Some plants have exploding seedpods that throw seeds into the air. Other seeds hitch a ride on humans or other animals that walk by. Have you ever found a bur on your sock after a walk in a field? The bur is actually the fruit of a plant. It has hooks that cling to you. When you brush it off, the bur falls to the ground giving the seeds inside a chance to grow.

Burs

Fighting in Place

Plants can't just get up and run away when they are threatened. So what do they do? They defend themselves in amazing ways.

The biggest problem for most plants is that animals like to eat them. So plants have developed special weapons for keeping animals away. Some plants have thorns or spines. For example, the ocotillo plant, pictured at lower right, is a thorny desert shrub that grows in the southwestern United States. Its branches are very spiny, so it doesn't offer an easy meal. In fact, the bush has such a good defense system that early settlers used ocotillo plants to make fences to keep their livestock penned in.

Sometimes plants use chemicals to protect themselves. If you've ever run into poison ivy, you know how this works. The itchy rash on your skin may last for many days—but you'll probably admit it's a good way for the plant to protect itself.

The stings of the nettle plant, pictured at right, also provide an unforgettable experience. When an animal rubs against the nettle, the stinging hairs prick like tiny needles. Then they release chemicals that can cause an unpleasant reaction— and animals learn to stay away.

The western buttercup, pictured at far right, is a bright yellow flower that looks pretty and seems harmless. Animals that eat it quickly learn that the flower has a very bad taste. It also contains a weak poison that makes animals sick. They don't often come back to this plant for a second helping.

Poison ivy

Nettle plant

Western buttercup

Ocotillo plant

Chapter 3

Products From Plants

The Sky's the Limit

What a strange sight! Are these scientists stuck? How did they get up there? What are they doing up above the trees?

Scientists aboard rain forest canopy raft

It's not a hot air balloon ride that ended badly. The scientists are actually hard at work studying the plants that grow in the **canopy**—the very top level of a rain forest. Rain forests are one of the richest environments on Earth. They are home to millions of species of plants and animals. The red research raft provides scientists with a platform from which to study life in the treetops. Scientists can even sleep on the raft, so they can stay up in the treetops for days at a time.

Rain forests cover only about 6 percent of Earth's land surface. However, they contain more than half of the plant species on Earth. Many of these plants provide useful medicines to use against human diseases. In fact, about 25 percent of prescription medicines in the United States are based on chemicals from rain forest plants. Scientists think that many new medicines might be developed from plants that are yet to be discovered.

Unfortunately, rain forests are disappearing. Rain forest trees are being cut down for lumber. Huge chunks of the forests are cleared to provide land for cattle and crops. Scientists haven't even identified all the plants in these forests yet. Some scientists think thousands of species of plants that we'll never even know about are being destroyed each year.

The spiny wood louse lives in the rain forest.

The Business of Plants

You know that plants are important because they provide us with oxygen, medicine, and shelter as well as food. Oats and corn are among the world's leading food crops, both for humans and livestock. Nearly one-third of all cropland worldwide is planted in wheat. In Asia, rice is the staple, or main food, of most people's diet.

From remote logging operations to downtown flower shops, many people earn their living producing products from plants. Thousands of products are made from plants —everything from hockey sticks to perfume. Look around you. Wooden furniture, books, and bed linens all are products made from plants.

What else do you use that might come from a plant?

Promising Future

In addition to looking for new medicines that plants might provide, researchers also study how plants can help clean the air. Some plants absorb certain **pollutants**, or harmful substances, from the air. We may be able to breathe a bit easier just by having the right plants around us.

The National Aeronautics and Space Administration (NASA) is interested in growing plants in space.

These baskets and hats are made from plant materials.

Astronaut Chiaki Mukai in space shuttle *Columbia* with bean sprouts growing in a cassette case

Astronauts in the International Space Station orbiting Earth are close enough to be supplied with food. But if we ever take a really long journey into space, we may need to grow plants along the way.

This presents problems. During space travel, the pull of gravity is generally not felt as strongly as it is here on Earth. This makes it difficult to sense which way is up or down. Plant roots usually need to grow down toward water and minerals. Plant stems and leaves grow toward light, which is usually up. Without a consistent light source and the pull of gravity, plants might not grow. Scientists are working on new ways to grow plants in space. Special growth chambers provide artificial light, controlled temperatures, and other things plants need. NASA scientists are also experimenting with **hydroponics**, a process for growing plants without soil. In a hydroponic environment, plants take up nutrients from the water in which they grow.

As you can see, plants are an essential part of our lives. In fact, we couldn't live without them.

Nature's Medicine Chest

Some plants offer more than food and beauty. People discovered long ago that certain plants help cure human ailments. Scientists are still looking for more remedies. Every year thousands of plants are examined in the search.

▲ **Cayenne pepper**
The spicy component in this plant is used to treat pain in joints.

◀ **Eucalyptus**
The oil from the leaves of this tree can be used to treat colds and flu.

▲ **Purple coneflower**
Native Americans used this plant to treat insect bites, toothaches, and burns.

Rosy periwinkle
Two drugs that come
from this plant can treat
some cancers.

Foxglove
Its leaves contain a chemical
called digitalis that is used to
treat heart conditions.

Fennel
Seeds can aid in digestion.

Garlic
Since the time
of the ancient
Egyptians, garlic
has been used
to treat a variety
of ailments.

**Scarlet
bergamot**
Dentists use
this as an
antiseptic to
fight germs.

Be smart. Don't ever eat any
parts of a wild plant. Some
plant substances that
normally help a person can
be harmful if taken in the
wrong amount. Some plants
can be poisonous.

Observing

Observation is an important skill when you're thinking like a scientist. When you look at something closely, you notice all of its features in detail.

An important product called Velcro was developed as a result of close observation. In the 1940s Swiss engineer George de Mestral was pulling plant burs from his pants and his dog's fur. He wondered why the burs attached so easily to his clothes. Looking closely under a microscope, he saw that each bur had hundreds of little hooks. He got the idea for a fastening device—and Velcro was born. Made up of loops and hooks that hold together, these fasteners have been used for decades in clothing, in medical and sports equipment, and more.

Practice the Skill

Use your powers of observation to examine the parts of the two flowers shown on page 27. Then see if you can answer the questions.

Focus On   Elizabeth Britton: Botanist

Elizabeth Britton always loved science. Born in New York City in 1858, she soon moved to Cuba, where her family lived on a sugar plantation. Britton attended schools in both Cuba and New York. As she got older, she decided to study botany—the science of plants. Britton became an expert on mosses. In 1902 she founded the Wildflower Preservation Society of America. She led movements that saved many endangered wildflower species. Britton also took the lead in establishing the New York Botanical Garden. Her vision brought a beautiful and educational garden right into the middle of New York City.

1. Find the stamens and pistil on each flower. How are they different?

2. In some flowers the sepals and petals look alike and are called tepals. Look at the base of each flower. Does the flower have sepals or tepals?

Flower 1
(back and front views)

Flower 2
(front and back views)

Check It Out

In some flowers the stamens are taller than the pistil. How do you think this might help a plant during pollination?

How Plants Respond to Light

As you know, plants need light to grow and make food. But can they actually grow through a maze to find light? To find out the answer, try this activity. It will take a couple of weeks of careful observation. Try to set up the project in a place where you will remember to check it every couple of days.

Materials
- ✔ Scissors
- ✔ Tape
- ✔ Ruler
- ✔ Large rubber band
- ✔ Cardboard shoe box with lid
- ✔ Cardboard dividers
- ✔ Four dry lima beans that have been soaked in water overnight
- ✔ Small flowerpot filled with dirt; pot must fit inside shoe box
- ✔ Safety goggles

SAFETY TIP: Always wear your safety goggles when you use scissors.

Explore

1. Design a simple maze by taping dividers inside the box. (*See photograph A.*)

2. Cut a 5-centimeter round hole in the lid of the box in the upper right corner. (*See photograph B.*)

3. Plant four beans in the flowerpot by pushing them gently underneath the surface of the dirt.

4. Put the pot in the corner that is farthest from the hole in the lid. (*See photograph C.*)

5. Put the lid on the box and secure it by putting the rubber band around the covered box.

6. Place the box in a sunny or well-lit location.

7. Over the next two weeks, open the box every two or three days. Water the beans if necessary to keep the dirt damp. Observe what is happening.

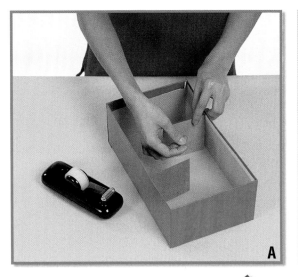

A

B

C

Think

At the end of two weeks, what do you observe? What do you think made the bean plants grow the way they did?

Science Notebook

AMAZING PLANT FACTS

- A single fully grown maple tree has about 150,000 leaves. That's a lot of raking!

- The flowers of the rafflesia plant, which grows in Southeast Asia, can grow to be roughly 1 meter (about 3 feet) wide.

- The largest seed in the world is the seed of the double coconut palm. A single seed can weigh about 23 kilograms (50 pounds).

- The smallest flowering plant in the world is the duckweed plant. Up to 50 of its flowers can fit into a space 2.5 centimeters (1 inch) long—each smaller than the head of a pin. Duckweed grows very rapidly and can quickly cover a pond.

- Bristlecone pines are among the world's oldest living trees. The oldest known bristlecone is about 4,800 years old. Bristlecones grow very slowly.

BOOKS TO READ

Akeroyd, John. *3D Eyewitness: Plant*. Dorling Kindersley Publishing, 1998.

Johnson, Rebecca L. *A Walk in the Rain Forest*. Carolrhoda Books, 2000.

WEBSITE TO VISIT

Gardening for Kids: *www.gardening launchpad.com/kids.html*

Rafflesia plant, Borneo Island

Glossary

canopy – the top layer of the rain forest

chlorophyll (*KLORE-uh-fill*) – the substance in leaves that gives them their green color and traps energy from the sun

conifer – a seed plant that produces seeds in cones

evergreen – a tree that has leaves all year long, shedding a small number of leaves throughout the year

fertilization – in plants, the combination of sperm from a pollen grain with an egg to form a seed

fibrous root system – kind of root system that spreads out into the surrounding soil

flowering plant – a seed plant that produces seeds in flowers and fruits

fruit – the part of a flowering plant that contains the seed or seeds

hydroponics – a process for growing plants without soil

nectar – a sweet liquid made in a flower that attracts insects and other animals

observe – use one or more of the five senses to gather information

petal – the often colorful part of a flower that surrounds the pistil and stamen

photosynthesis (*foh-toh-SIN-thuh-sis*) – plant process that uses energy from sunlight to make food

pistil – the part of a flower that produces egg cells

pollen – tiny grains that produce sperm, which combine with a flower's egg cells to make seeds

pollination – process in which pollen is moved from a stamen to a pistil of a flower

pollutant – harmful substance in the air, soil, or water

respiration – energy-releasing process that generally uses oxygen and gives off carbon dioxide

sepal – leaflike part that protects the bud of a flowering plant

spore – tiny reproductive structure of ferns and mosses

stamen – the part of a flower that makes pollen

taproot – a straight, thick main root that grows down into the soil

woody stem – stem of trees and shrubs

Index